LISTEN WITH YOUR HEART

Five-Minute Meditations

William F. McKee, C.SS.R.

LIGUORI
PUBLICATIONS

One Liguori Drive
Liguori, Missouri 63057
(314) 464-2500

Imprimi Potest:
Stephen T. Palmer, C.SS.R.
Provincial, St. Louis Province
Redemptorist Fathers

Imprimatur:
+ Edward J. O'Donnell
Vicar General, Archdiocese of St. Louis

ISBN 0-89243-270-5
Library of Congress Catalog Card Number: 87-80217

Table of Contents

GUIDELINES

Introduction

As a priest I live in a sheltered cocoon. Some people call it an unreal world. Friends tell me I would be able to relate to them and their pain better if I were not so insulated.

As a priest I emerge from the cocoon to do my work. I preside at liturgies. I administer the sacraments. I preach. I teach. I visit the sick. I listen to people who are hurting. I conduct sessions for those who have left the Church. I have meetings for those who want to know more about God and his love. I do the hundred and one tasks that most other priests do.

As a priest, when my work is done I return to the rectory. Any problems I have there are minor. The major ones I have left outside. This does not mean that I do not hurt with those who hurt and ache with those who ache. But my ache, my pain, does not have their depth or width or height. Theirs is sleeping next to them in bed or in the crib across the hall or in their teenager's room or over in their parents' home or in the house of a dear friend.

As a priest I see both advantage and disadvantage in my insulation. The advantage is that I am not so involved in their pain that I lose my objectivity and sense of direction. The disadvantage is that I don't want them to hurt any more than I do. And they do — with spouses, with children, with intimate relationships, with financial worries, with concern about old age, with doubts about salvation itself. Although I have my own problems, none of them can compare to theirs. I just don't have to worry about the thousand and one things that disrupt their days and cause sleepless nights. They live in their world; I live in mine.

As a priest, if someone I love dies, my life is not outwardly changed. True, I weep as someone who loves. I know that an important part of me is gone forever, but my lifestyle goes on unchanged.

As a priest, when I stand next to the coffin of a young mother, I feel helpless and inadequate in the presence of her husband and children. Long ago I gave up mouthing clichés: "It's God's will," or "God loved her more than you did." All I can do is hug and hold and pray. Only those who have been through similar deaths can relate to the pain in the family's hearts.

As a priest I really don't know what to say to the young mother whose fifteen-year-old unmarried daughter is pregnant. But I have seen mothers who have been through the situation with their own daughters and who know exactly what to say and do. I watch them admiringly and wish I could be as tenderly helpful.

As a priest I tell a man his sins are forgiven him and they are forgiven. He walks away with a new heart and a clean slate. As he leaves I think of what God has done. A divine event has taken place through me. I stand in adoring awe of the Lord who made it happen.

As a priest I pour baptismal water over a baby and know the little one will never be the same again. Through God's words and my actions, new life begins.

As a priest I have often been asked if I feel anything when I pronounce the words of consecration at Mass that turn the bread and wine into the body and blood of Christ. I do. Sometimes I am overcome by what is happening and I feel dizzy with emotion and a kind of believing disbelief that I am participating in such a miracle. That our great God would be so interested in us weak and imperfect mortals is hard to understand. But he *is* interested and there is nothing in the world that compares to it.

As a priest there are many things I cannot do. But I can try to relate better to people, understand their problems, help them get through their transitions of pain. My desire is to do what I can to make people feel that their priest is at their side, that he really cares. And that is the purpose of the following meditations.

Be Glad You're
God's Child

During my early days of study for the priesthood, I was disappointed to learn that God does not laugh at jokes. God cannot be taken by surprise; he knows all the punch lines.

The professors assured me that although God does not actually laugh, he is very happy. He possesses the fullness of happiness and never has a bad day. That was reassuring. I did not want the one who runs the world to get depressed.

Well, I asked myself, if God the Father does not laugh, maybe his Son did. But nowhere in the New Testament does it say that Jesus "laughed" or "smiled." Yet he must have laughed because, as the author of the Letter to the Hebrews wrote: "he had to become like his brothers in every way" (Hebrews 2:17). As an example, he certainly must have welcomed with a smile the little children brought to him for his blessing.

That God is happy and wants us to be happy even in this life, that Jesus smiled and laughed and went around healing people so they could be happy, does not seem to appeal to some people. Their picture of God is etched with lines of severity. They see him as one who is unhappy with his creatures and is just waiting to strike them down — for their sins, perhaps even for their smiles and laughter.

It is such people who seem to think that this life is supposed to be as much of a hell as possible so that hell in the next life will be avoided.

But Jesus says, "I assure you, unless you change and become like little children, you will not enter the kingdom of God" (Matthew 18:3).

Children, all things being equal, are happy persons. They giggle, they laugh, they have fun, they enjoy life, they live each moment as if there were no tomorrow. Jesus tells us to be like them.

Forgiven sinners frequently feel they haven't been punished enough for their sins; and if, perchance, they begin to enjoy life, they think something must be wrong.

Life is hard enough without such heresy. While the Bible and the Church offer severe admonitions about doing good and avoiding evil, nowhere is it said that anyone, including forgiven sinners, should have a hell on earth.

The Ten Commandments, the Beatitudes, and the sacraments bring us happiness in this life. The sacrament of Penance conveys us pure and unspotted to God the Father. It prepares us for the union that takes place in the Eucharist. It takes us up to heaven even though our feet never leave the earth. The Eucharist is definite proof that God loves us unconditionally.

Once, in speaking to and of fathers of families, Jesus said: "If you, with all your sins, know how to give your children what is good, how much more will your heavenly Father give good things to anyone who asks him!" (Matthew 7:11)

And so our job is to ask. Then we will receive the goodness that brings happiness.

We are God's own children. Therefore we should lift high our heads with joy and stretch out our arms with gladness, assuring him that we are happy. No father wants his children to be sad.

Say Yes to God and His People

Saying yes to God and his people is a good thing.

Saying yes to God is adoration.
It's awareness.
It's understanding.
It's prayer.
It's reassurance.
It's faith.

Worry
Pain
Loss
Inhumanity
Betrayal
Sin
Lack of concern
Indifference
Horror
    tend to tie the yessing tongue.
Tied tongues can always be untied.

Peace
Grace
Glory
    follow.

People too need yesses.
All the time.
People need to know that they are worthwhile.
Yes reassures them.

People are weak.
Yes supplies strength.

Saying yes may be

>   a nod
>   a smile
>   a tear
>   a being there
>
>   a hand
>   a loving
>   a walking with
>   a talking to
>   a listening
>   a saying no.

Where people end and God begins is hard to see.
Ofttimes God and people are the same.

Dapple each day with yesses.
Greet morn and eve with a yes.

Saying yes is godliness.

Don't Try to Remake God

God tells us quite clearly in the first book of the Bible that he made us in his own image and likeness (see Genesis 1:26-27). Nowhere does the Bible or the Church even hint that we are to shape God after our own image. The Israelites, as we read in the Book of Exodus, made a calf of gold for their worship, and God punished them for their idolatry (see Exodus 32:1-35).

"Remaking" God is still quite common in today's world. For example, even though God has made it clear that no sin is too great to be forgiven, the person wanting forgiveness may still say, "My sins are too great for God to forgive."

In the parable of the Prodigal Son, the son decides to go back home, saying: "I will break away and return to my father, and say to him, Father, I have sinned against God and against you; I no longer deserve to be called your son. Treat me like one of your hired hands" (Luke 15:18-19).

However, the people who try to remake God say, "We cannot return to our Father because he would not want us back. We no longer deserve to be called his children. We gave up our birthrights when we broke his law."

Actually, in the parable the father welcomes back his son with the words, "Let us eat and celebrate because this son of mine was dead and has come back to life. He was lost and is found" (Luke 15:23-24).

Still, some will say, "I find that hard to believe. I dare say the prodigal son never committed as many sins as I have. That father would never receive me back."

Such words do an injustice to God by assigning human attributes to a divine Being.

When I was a young priest, I was always edified by our older Redemptorist missionaries. It was said of them that they were lions in the pulpit (preaching the eternal truths with great force and vigor) but

11

lambs in the confessional (treating sinners with compassion, tenderness, and acceptance).

I talked with several of them about this because I wanted to be like them. I asked them how they could be so understanding of sinners. They told me that one day I would understand.

Today I do understand. Today I know that all God wants from us is a humble and contrite heart. "A heart contrite and humbled, O God, you will not spurn" (Psalm 51:19).

God is big — wonderfully, lovingly big. We are little — wonderfully, lovingly little. Don't try, then, to remake him into your own image.

Find God
in People

In the early years of my religious life I tended to place more emphasis on God than on people. To have a strong friendship with God through the sacraments and prayer was my number one priority. My family, relatives, and friends occupied a slightly lower place on my scale of values. People came in second.

Today, after more than thirty years in the priesthood, it seems clear to me that both God and people come first. In one sense it is difficult to see where one stops and the other begins.

An extraordinary statement in the First Letter of John emphasizes this fact very forcefully.

"If we love one another
God dwells in us" (1 John 4:12).

Our love for each other brings God down from heaven to live in us. It is awesome to think that human love knocks at the door of divinity and says "Come abide with me" — and divinity obeys.

In Matthew 25:31-46, Jesus points out the effect that human relationships have on him. The scene is the Last Judgment, where he tells those who will inherit the kingdom: "I was hungry and you gave me food, I was thirsty and you gave me drink. . . . " On being asked when they did these things, Jesus answers: "As often as you did it for one of my least brothers, you did it for me." And the opposite is, of course, true: When we abuse, manipulate, or use for unholy ends another human being, we do it to Jesus.

At times, most of us wonder how we are getting along with God. Is he pleased or displeased with us? We find the answer to that question by examining our relationships with people. If we are getting along well with people in a loving way — or trying to do so — we are getting along well with him.

"One who has no love for the brother he has seen
cannot love the God he has not seen" (1 John 4:20).

Our relationship with people is a yardstick to measure our relationship with God. Jesus goes to great lengths to emphasize this point: "If you bring your gift to the altar and there recall that your brother has anything against you, leave your gift at the altar, go first to be reconciled with your brother, and then come and offer your gift" (Matthew 5:23-24).

Evidently God wants us to be involved with the sticky, frequently messy, and difficult problems that arise in human relationships and to work through them in order to come to him. There is to be no skirting the issue, no bypassing people in our many life situations. It is easy to deceive ourselves about how we are relating to our God if we avoid people. The daily nose-to-nose and soul-to-soul confrontations that come as we live with people leave little room for self-deception.

In the booklet *Spiritual Renewal of the American Priesthood*, we read the following: "No man is an island; each owes his being and his becoming, his self-understanding and his self-love, to the people who bring him life." People give other people a second, third, and fourth birth.

Still, this approach to God through people does not mean we are never to approach him directly. Private prayer must be an intimate part of our lives. Jesus himself frequently left the disciples and went off alone into the desert to pray. And he tells his disciples: "Whenever you pray, go to your room, close your door, and pray to your Father in private. Then your Father, who sees what no man sees, will repay you" (Matthew 6:6).

Whenever we are in contact with people, there is always the possibility that problems will arise. But it is in people and their problems that we find the beauty and the riches of God himself.

To Become Secure, Learn to Love

The future is God's private property and we should not invade it by excessive worrying.

For many years of my life I followed that principle. I set my worries aside, entrusting them to the Lord. But as I grew older I began to fret again. I worried about my work, about my health, about where I would be working, about getting to heaven. I knew I was wrong to worry but I couldn't help it. I wanted my future to be secure. I wanted to be in control of my life, to have the assurance that my last years would be peaceful ones. I thought it was up to me to make it happen. I became miserable.

When I look back I can see colossal egoism on my part. Why should I be secure when no one else is? Why should I have a lock on the future when such is not possible?

What helped bring me to my senses was a reading from Romans: "None of us lives as his own master and none of us dies as his own master. . . . Both in life and in death we are the Lord's" (Romans 14:7-8). That sentence overwhelmed me because I was basically trying to live as my own master, to be in control.

As I looked around I saw that no one really has complete control of his or her own life. We have health today, and tomorrow we get bad news from the doctor. We have a good home today, and tomorrow Hurricane Mabel wipes it out. We have a good job today, and tomorrow we get a pink slip. So goes life.

President Ronald Reagan and Pope John Paul II probably realize the full force of what I write more than you or I. If their would-be assassins' bullets had struck vital organs, neither would have lived.

Security can be found only in Jesus Christ. Outside of Jesus there is nothing permanent, nothing solid to stand on. All is shifting sand. Jesus is rock.

"There is no Holy One like the LORD;
there is no Rock like our God" (1 Samuel 2:2).

How do we make that rock the foundation of our security? There is only one way — by learning to LOVE. The person who loves is secure. The non-lover, the one who cares for no one but self, is never secure. The lover, unlike the non-lover, stands on the rock with hands open to God and to people. Only when it is given away, Jesus said, can life be gained.

It is not easy to stand on that rock because it involves interaction with people. People are the measure of our love for God.

"If anyone says, 'My love is fixed on God,'
yet hates his brother,
he is a liar. . . .
Whoever loves God must also love his brother."
(1 John 4:20-21)

And we read further on in the same Letter:

"Whoever possesses the Son possesses life;
whoever does not possess the Son of God
does not possess life" (1 John 5:12).

In this our security rests.

Saint Paul spells out clearly the security that comes from loving: "For I am certain that neither death nor life, neither angels nor principalities, neither the present nor the future, nor powers, neither height nor depth nor any other creature, will be able to separate us from the love of God that comes to us in Christ Jesus, our Lord" (Romans 8:38-39).

So it's back to the drawing board for me. I will try to forget the future and remember people — their needs, their pains, their wanting to be heard, and their hunger for love. Only by learning to love will I find security.

Love
Yourself

An American priest traveling down a country road in Ireland met up with an old man and asked if he might walk with him. They sauntered along until rain forced them into a shelter. After a while, the old man took out a prayer book and began to pray. A beautiful look came over his face. The priest, seeing this, said to him, "You must be very close to God." The old man answered, "Yes, he is very fond of me."

Do you think God is very fond of you? Do you go to bed at night assured and happy that God likes you? If your answer is no, welcome to the human race. Many people think that God dislikes them or at most merely tolerates them.

Bad self-images show up in all classes of people — the rich, the poor; the successful, the unsuccessful; the achievers, the non-achievers; the powerful, the weak. There is no group that is exempt.

This is tragic as well as regrettable. The reason it is so sad is that if people do not think that God loves them, they will not be in a position to love themselves. It impairs their self-image and weakens their self-love. When self-love is undermined, people cannot adequately love their neighbor and, ultimately, their God. Jesus gave us basically two commandments: to love God and to love our neighbor as ourselves. If we do not love ourselves, how can we love our neighbor? We cannot give what we do not have. No doubt a vast amount of hatred shown in the world flows out of the inner streams of self-hatred within individuals.

Here are some reasons why some of us do not love ourselves and therefore cannot imagine that God is fond of us.

a) *We have a false idea of humility.* In humility we recognize not only our bad qualities but also our good ones. But some of us seem to think humility demands that we put ourselves down. One test of this is how we handle compliments. If we cannot accept a well-deserved compliment, we do not understand the importance of loving ourselves.

b) *We think that God cannot love us because we have sinned.* We worry about original sin (the tendency all people have toward evil) and about personal sin (which we ourselves commit). But original sin (forgiven at Baptism) was not our fault and our personal sins can also be forgiven. Our God is a God who forgives and forgets. Consider Mary Magdalen and Peter. They were great sinners who became close friends of Jesus.

c) *We view God as a cruel tyrant waiting to pounce on us for our least mistake.* But nowhere in the New Testament can we find justification for such an attitude. There we see that God is compassionate, tender, loving, and forgiving.

d) *We believe that everything material is bad.* Our bodies are bad and only our souls are good. Because of this we feel it is impossible to have our sins forgiven and we are certain that we are unworthy to receive Holy Communion. But this is the heresy of Manichaeism which long ago was condemned by the Church.

We should face the fact that we are splendid, beautiful creations made in the image and likeness of God (see Genesis 1:26). We have been made "little less than the angels" (Psalm 8:6) and have been redeemed by the blood of God's Son.

As believers in Christ we should have no problem with our self-image as we exult in being friends of God, beloved of Father, Son, and Holy Spirit.

We must then have proper love for ourselves; otherwise we will have little or no love of others. So never put yourself down. It is not the loving thing to do.

Listen With
a Loving Heart

In the early days of my priesthood, I thought Paul's statement in Romans, "Faith . . . comes through hearing," (10:17) referred only to listening to the Word of God.

It did not occur to me that faith could come from listening to the words of ordinary people: husbands, wives, friends, enemies, parents, and their teenage children. I judged faith to be so solemn and important that it was reserved only for solemn and important settings. But today I know better.

Father Henri Nouwen, in his book, *Intimacy,* writes, "Since God became man, man has become the main source of our understanding of God." Human beings can tell us of life and God. But we have to listen.

True listening implies that we get behind the words of the speaker. We hear not only with our ears but also with our eyes, heart, and mind.

This type of listening requires a degree of concentration that is hard to achieve. It is based on an unselfish and non-judgmental attitude which refrains from offering advice or solutions. Its main purpose is acceptance of the speaker. Those who listen in this way show complete interest in the other person. People are good listeners only to the extent that they somehow become one with the one who speaks.

Only a lover is capable of such listening. Lovers care; therefore they listen. The non-lover does not care and will not listen.

A lover seeks the good of the other person or the good of Christ or the good of the family of God and his kingdom through the other person. No one but a lover can do this.

Is listening worth the effort? Well, besides imparting and increasing faith within us, it also has a healing effect — for both speaker and listener. So often we say to ourselves: "I just had to talk to somebody." We need a listener — to ease our pain, to lessen our guilt, to show approval, to give acceptance. A good listener brings healing.

Part of the healing that takes place in the confessional is due simply to the fact that the confessor listens. Most priests are aware that good listening is required if they are to fulfill their role as *other Christs*.

The poet Rod McKuen — in a popular magazine article — tells of being cruelly raped by his uncle when he was a boy. He says that the scar has never healed because he kept it to himself for so long. His advice to those in similar circumstances: "Tell someone immediately." The telling will ease the pain and perhaps heal the scar.

What if he had told someone and that person did not listen? Imagine the horror such non-listening would create in a young boy.

So much pain and suffering could be avoided if people with similar hurts had someone to listen to them, someone who would say in a loving way, "Here I am. Talk to me and I will hear you out."

We ask God to listen to us. We pray, convinced he will. God in turn asks us to listen to each other. People have a right to be heard and we have a duty to listen. They have a claim on the listening-healing power within us. It is there for their good. We cannot use it for ourselves except through them.

These words from the Genesis II program pertain here: "Insofar as I tell you who I am, I am at the same time revealing part of the beauty of God." We have been created in the image and likeness of God. Soul-speaking and soul-listening let that image shine through. Listening affirms the God within us.

We must learn to listen to the inner pain, the aching of the soul, the wounds of the heart, the joys of loving and being alive. When we listen in this way we synchronize our heartbeat with the heartbeat of the other person. It tells us who that person is and makes us glad that we have listened with a loving heart.

Console
the Lonely

Mother Teresa of Calcutta once said that the greatest suffering in the world today is loneliness. She said too many people feel abandoned, forgotten, unwanted, rejected. These feelings cause a sense of loneliness that is as high as the mountains and as deep as the seas. It is a sorrow that wraps itself around the heart and squeezes out the blood of happiness.

Loneliness does not necessarily mean being alone. Many busy, active persons — surrounded by family, friends, and relatives — feel lonely. On the other hand, a person can be alone without ever suffering the pain of loneliness. It all depends on the state of mind.

Evidently some loneliness is good. It is part of God's plan to make us call out to him and to want him. Saint Augustine said, ''My heart is restless until it rests in thee.'' And Jesus himself expressed the fullness of loneliness in his cry from the Cross: ''My God, my God, why have you forsaken me?''

The saints, as they followed in the Master's footsteps, have gone through the same acute agony of loneliness. Saint Alphonsus, founder of the Redemptorists, said in his declining years, ''I am a bag of worms and I wonder why anyone bothers about me.''

Many beautiful, talented people are also lonely, even as their public admirers crowd around them. One such woman told me that beauty and talent can erect barriers between people. She said that she frequently felt isolated, then alone, then lonely. She wondered if her beauty and talent were, in the end, worth all the suffering and sorrow.

A recent article on the drug abuse among film and stage stars pointed out the emptiness of many public figures. Leaving the stage, the thunder of applause, and the sounds of approval, they return to a lonely hotel room and try to obliterate their pain and their emptiness with drugs and alcohol.

Often young people today fill their sense of loneliness by joining one of the many available cults. This was rather dramatically illustrated not too long ago when the Reverend Sun Myung Moon of the Church of the Unification presided at the wedding of two thousand couples in Madison Square Garden in New York.

Just what is the attraction that Moon and other cultists hold for the young? Why are they able to draw so many youngsters to them? How do they gain such complete control over them? Perhaps the most forceful answer to those questions is that the cults make young people feel wanted and needed. They are given a sense of importance, of belonging. And in the early indoctrinations given them, young people are led to believe that the rites of the cult are tailored to the individual, not the individual to the religion — even though later they learn otherwise.

Whenever I meet lonely people and they want to talk about their loneliness, to get some kind of help, I make only two suggestions: Get involved with the Bible and seek out another lonely person.

Reading the Bible and going to Bible classes (which are springing up all over the country in Catholic parishes) have a tremendous impact on loneliness. This is no doubt due to the fact that the Bible makes the reader feel the presence and the interest and the love of God more than any other single factor. And when the Bible is studied together with other people, the presence of the Lord is felt even more profoundly. "Where two or three are gathered in my name, there am I in their midst" (Matthew 18:20).

The other great antidote for loneliness is to seek out another lonely person and try to make that person feel better. The sick, the widowed, the orphaned, the separated, the divorced — these are all possible candidates for loneliness. But the symptoms can be found in countless persons in today's world.

Loneliness is indeed a great suffering, as Mother Teresa said. Some of it can be good, but most of it should be eliminated. And we should thank God that through his goodness and love we have the ability to console the lonely.

Pray for the Gift of Compassion

Lord, things are tough out there. The world's a mess. Every day brings more reports of war, hijacking, violence, child abuse, earthquakes, floods, hurricanes, rapes. People are scared. They're putting locks on the doors of their lives. And there's a lot of pain that doesn't make the headlines. Really, Lord, something has to be done.

When you were around, you took care of a lot of suffering. Most of the time you were either healing or on your way to heal or just returning from a healing. You wanted people to be healthy and happy not only in heaven but also on earth.

Dear Lord, what would you do for these people who have recently come into my life?

1. The mother came home from the hospital with her ninth child. She was glowing. The new baby girl was a beauty, like all her other children. When she walked into the house, the first words she heard were, "Daddy's gone and he isn't coming back." There was a note — "I'm leaving you. A lawyer will contact you about a divorce."

2. The man was backing out of his driveway, worried sick about whether he was going to get fired or not. The company was cutting back. How was he going to break the news to his wife and children if he was fired? He felt his back wheel hit something. It was his three-year-old son. He had run over the boy and killed him. . . . And the same day he found out he had been fired.

3. She had become so depressed that she had to be confined in restraints at the state mental hospital so she wouldn't kill herself. Her husband sits by her side, hour after hour, and throbs with pain big enough to fill an ocean.

Lord, we know that you would have shown compassion to these good people. You would have made them feel that their pain was yours, too. You would have healed them of all or part of the hurt.

Lord, we want to be like you. As compassionate people we recognize the deep pain and hurt of others. Your wounded children count on us to bring them your compassionate healing. But often we feel ineffective. We would like to do more but don't know how.

Lord Jesus, we know that pain has existed since the beginning. From what we see around us, we feel that there is more today than ever before. Would you please do something about it? You yourself said, "Ask and you shall receive. Knock and it shall be opened to you."

We ask. We knock. We pray. We know that you gave us the Church and the sacraments to help us handle life and death. But since life is moving at such a hurting pace these days, we need more help.

Your kind of compassion, Lord, will make these people feel human again. It will restore their sense of worth and their confidence in you. It will let them know that you never abandoned them and that you love them still.

O Lord, help us to show the same kind of compassion displayed in the healing power of the sacraments of Baptism, Penance, and Anointing.

Lord, teach all of us — priests, religious, and laity — to heal and to help others in their time of need. And if healing is not what you want at the moment, then give us the patience to listen with love to those who are hurting. Show us how to let them know we are aware of how much they are hurting. Give us the gift of compassion.

Weep With
Those Who Weep

Failure to become involved with the pain of others is a difficulty that many people have in today's world. As a priest, in the past I thought I had enough pain of my own without taking on more. I would listen to people's suffering or heartache with great attention. I would pray with and for them, perhaps advise them, console them as best I could, and then let them go without allowing any of their pain to touch me personally.

Today I realize how wrong I was. I understand now that my life and theirs would have been richer, fuller, if I, like Christ, had been ready to commiserate with others.

Christ did more than cure, raise from the dead, pity the crowds who "were like sheep without a shepherd" (Mark 6:34). He even took into himself the pain of an entire city: "Coming within sight of the city [Jerusalem], he wept over it . . . " (Luke 19:41).

Jesus also wept over Lazarus. "When Jesus saw her [Mary] weeping, and the Jews who had accompanied her also weeping, he was troubled in spirit, moved by the deepest emotions . . . [and] Jesus began to weep" (John 11:33,35). The loving, tenderhearted interaction between Jesus, Mary, Martha, and Lazarus is one of the most consoling stories of the New Testament.

Commiseration is a virtue with many faces. It is a sharing with the pain of those who have suffered failure or brokenness or fear or anxiety. It can mean that we weep with those who weep, that we take on loneliness to be with those who are lonely, that we become weak for the sake of those who are weak. It is something we do without measuring the cost or worrying about the time. The commiserative are not just those persons in the lifeboat throwing life preservers to those drowning in the ocean; they are in the ocean themselves, helping the others into the boat or to the safety of the shore.

A recent book, *Compassion,* by McNeil, Morrison, and Nouwen, points to patience as an effective means of practicing compassion or commiseration. "Patience counteracts our unreflective impulse to flee or fight." For those of us who have given in to this impulse when we should have shown sympathy, that sentence makes a lot of sense.

Patience means giving up control, entering unknown territory. It urges us to step out of self and into the being of the other person who is broken. It demands that we shed a part of ourselves. This is not easy to do.

A priest said to me recently, "I think that my impatience is a form of selfishness. I simply don't have the patience to tolerate or bear with people and their pain as I should. Yet I want them to be patient with me."

There are two kinds of people who have the patience to express this kind of sympathy: lovers and pray-ers. Those who have concentrated on loving others will be commiserative without a second thought. Those who are not outwardly friendly by nature need to pray for this virtue.

Acts of kindness in the form of commiseration do not come naturally to everyone. But we can ask God for this precious gift. And with God's help we can learn to be sympathetic toward others.

Almighty God took pity on the fallen human race and sent his own Son to redeem the world. He did this by dying on the Cross. But the Cross led to glory:

"Because of this [Christ's death on the Cross],
    God highly exalted him
    and bestowed on him the name
    above every other name" (Philippians 2:9).

When we Christians weep with those who weep here on earth, we prepare ourselves for the eternal joys of heaven.

QUESTIONS

Are You Happy?

I have spent the greater part of my sixty-odd years on earth believing that tears, rather than laughter, were what life is all about; that we were created more to be unhappy than happy. I felt sure that the curses God put on Adam and the whole human race (woman shall give birth in pain; man must earn his living by the sweat of his brow; all will taste death) were indications that God was so angry at us that he did not want us to be happy except for short periods of time.

Today I know that I was wrong. Today I realize with all the force of my being that God *does* want us to be happy, that this world is a preparation for the next world, that God's kingdom begins right here on earth.

These were conclusions I reached in reading the New Testament. Why would Jesus work the miracle at Cana — changing water into wine — unless it was to make the guests and newlyweds happy? Why did Jesus heal if not to make suffering people healthy and happy? "People brought him all the afflicted, with the plea that he let them do no more than touch the tassel of his cloak. As many as touched it were fully restored to health" (Matthew 14:35-36).

Jesus suffered when people suffered. He suffered with them in order to lessen their pain. "At the sight of the crowds, his heart was moved with pity" (Matthew 9:36). And later, "When he . . . saw the vast throng, his heart was moved with pity, and he cured their sick" (Matthew 14:14).

The teaching of Jesus is founded on a profound desire for people to be happy. The Sermon on the Mount (in which we find the Beatitudes) is a beautiful example of what Jesus desires for all of us:

"How blest are the poor in spirit:
the reign of God is theirs.
Blest too are the sorrowing; they shall be consoled.
[Blest are the lowly; they shall inherit the land] . . ."
(Matthew 5:3-5).

Jesus certainly did not want to eliminate all pain and sorrow. Pain can be a great teacher and, strangely enough, a great healer. It can teach us that God is with us and for us, and it can heal the wounds opened by selfishness.

Although God does not will us to be in pain, when pain comes through natural causes, he can use it to make us better persons. Pain can be called the crooked line with which God writes straight.

Another conviction I have today that I did not have twenty years ago is that we are just about as happy as we really want to be. So much of our happiness depends upon us. Outside forces or persons cannot infiltrate the inner sanctum of our being where happiness is made and stored. Only we can. We are our own happiness-makers. And the greatest and simplest way to make ourselves happy is to make others happy — to give others the love or signs of esteem, affection, and affirmation they need to be happy.

Because many people feel doomed to unhappiness, they do not pray for happiness. They feel unworthy of this great favor. But happiness is a right to which all of us have a claim. Jesus promises us:

"Ask and you shall receive,
that your joy may be full" (John 16:24).

We were not born to weep. We were made for laughter. And with God's help, we will sing in concert with the psalmist:

"You changed my mourning into dancing;
you took off my sackcloth and clothed me with gladness"
(Psalm 30:12).

Yes, God wants us to be happy.

Are You
Afraid to Love?

She seemed to be a very loving person. The way she related to her husband and children indicated that. So I asked her my question: "Do you think most people are afraid to love?" She answered, without hesitation, "Yes, of course. Real love is not easy to maintain."

Hard facts prove the woman right. In spite of all the joy, the ecstacy, the fulfillment of loving and being loved, most people are afraid of the involvement that comes with love.

The New Testament alone has over 124 exhortations to love. And out of love, Jesus died for us. Why, then, don't we love him in return? There are many reasons.

Selfishness is one. Love demands that we give ourselves away even though this means a loss of our freedom.

Fear is another. We are afraid of exposing our secret selves and also of being rejected. Rejection leaves us feeling valueless; and self-revelation horrifies us because we do not want to be seen as we really are.

Our *pride* also keeps us from loving. We think so much of ourselves that imperfect human beings are not quite worthy of us.

Selfishness, fear, and pride are unworthy reasons for being afraid to love. We know that human love requires constant dialoguing, caring, listening, and forgiving.

Saint Paul reminds us that love is patient, kind, humble, and unselfish (see 1 Corinthians 13:4-7). He exhorts us not to pass off as love that which is not love. Here are some examples:

Gratitude is not love. To repay others for what they do for us is not love. People just want to be loved for what they actually are.

Mutual sexual satisfaction is not necessarily love. Such satisfaction is present in a loving relationship; but other factors — like tenderness — are needed for true love.

Fulfillment of a need to be loved is not really love. Need cannot be the foundation for a loving relationship because when the need no longer exists, love disappears.

Jealousy which excludes everyone but the beloved is not true love. True love for one person establishes a character trait which makes us love others too.

Possessiveness is not a sign of love. An old adage reads: "If you love something, set it free. If it returns, it's yours. If it doesn't, it never was." And Leo Buscaglia writes, "If you close your arms around love, you will find you are left holding only yourself."

Reformers are not genuine lovers. Trying to change the habits of others to make them better is certainly not a form of love.

Real love is a meeting of souls on common ground. In popular language the word *hearts* is used here instead of souls. In philosophy the will is the love center (or seat) and is part of our spiritual nature, just as the intellect (mind) is part of our spiritual nature.

Whatever language we use for the seat of love, most of us understand the symbolism of the heart. We show the love between two people as hearts entwined. And when we bring God into the picture — as we must — three hearts are entwined. He brings power, strength, and durability to human love in the sacrament of Matrimony. This faith-filled and hope-filled triangle of God and two persons makes for perfect love.

Jesus insists that love is necessary to bring his kingdom here on earth in preparation for eternity. Scripture leaves no doubt about this: We are called to love.

But love is impossible without self-discipline. Those who discipline themselves to obey the commandments are the ones who love him (see John 14:21). This is so because of the following sequence: *Self-discipline is the basis for self-respect; self-respect is necessary for self-love; self-love is necessary for love of neighbor; and love of neighbor is necessary for love of God.*

So, if we are willing to practice self-discipline, we will never be afraid to love.

Do You Have
the Spirit of Christ?

Recently I was struck by a statement Saint Paul made in his Letter to the Romans (8:9): "If anyone does not have the Spirit of Christ, he does not belong to Christ." These words made me wonder whether my life manifested the spirit of Christ.

Then I grew angry at Saint Paul and asked: "How in the world can I have the spirit of the God-man? That's impossible!"

Bellowing at Saint Paul made me feel good until a voice within me said, *The spirit of Christ urges you to let go and never give up.* That made me groan because, like most people, I want to be in personal control of my life and my destiny.

Evidently Paul (who is a pretty crafty fellow) knew what I was thinking because he reminded me of his words in that same Letter to the Romans (14:7-8): "None of us lives as his own master and none of us dies as his own master. . . . Both in life and in death we are the Lord's."

If I am the Lord's, how much of me is mine? Not much, according to Jesus' own words. "He who seeks only himself brings himself to ruin, whereas he who brings himself to nought for me discovers who he is" (Matthew 10:39).

So this was the investment he sought: I give up me and get him. Quite an exchange, I must say. But can I live as a child of the Lord? I could try, I thought.

So I began to look around me with a new awareness. I saw more clearly that living is a strange and remarkable affair. Today I am in control; tomorrow I am not. It doesn't take long to go from the warmth of love and success to the chill of pain and failure.

I know and you know, of course, that God is ever-ready to comfort. "Come to me, all you who are weary and find life burdensome, and I will refresh you . . . for I am gentle and humble of heart. Your souls will find rest, for my yoke is easy and my burden light'' (Matthew 11:28-30).

Such reassurance from God helps you to hang in there and not give up. Giving up is the easy way. It is not easy to repeat the words of Jesus: ''My Father, if it is possible, let this cup pass me by. Still, let it be as you would have it, not as I'' (Matthew 26:39).

The message of Jesus is clear: Don't give up!

Don't give up on God. Know that he allows evil to happen; but he is author and giver only of that which is good.

Don't give up on your relationships. There may be pain in your marriage or certain friendships; but pain can be a purifier and a builder, so don't waste it. At times you may be tempted to walk away, saying you can do better elsewhere. Then you see Jesus out of the corner of your eye, shaking his head and saying: ''That is not my way; that is not my spirit.'' Recall his relationship with Peter. In spite of the pain that Peter's denial must have caused him, he never gave up on the leader of his apostles.

Don't give up on prayer. It may seem that God is not listening, but he is just waiting for you to let go so he can come in.

Don't give up on yourself. You are not so bad that a good God would not like to have you around. Remember the great sinners God loved — people like Peter and Mary Magdalen. This is what he thought of repentant sinners: He made Peter the head of his Church and he gave Magdalen the privilege of being the first to see him after he rose from the dead. Because they never gave up on themselves, Jesus never gave up on them. Contrast their stories with the story of Judas. He gave up on himself and ended up hanging from a tree.

In my many years of priesthood, it has been my experience that more people have the spirit of Christ than is apparent. So, if Saint Paul walks into your life and asks, ''Do you have the spirit of Christ?'' you can rightfully answer back, ''Yes, I belong to him!''

Do You Hunger
for Peace and Goodness?

He was a big, burly, mean-looking man. When he came in the room for our session with inactive Catholics, I said to myself, "I hope this man isn't angry at priests." I handed him our standard newcomer form to fill out. On the paper is the question, "What would you like to get out of this meeting?"

Without hesitation, he wrote "Peace of mind." He handed me the paper with the look of a man who was desperate. Somehow I sensed that he had sought peace in many other places and had not found it. His appearance here, I suspected, was his last resort. I was deeply touched.

In the years that followed that incident, hundreds of people have written that same word on their papers: PEACE.

Many of them have also written another word: GOODNESS. They added things like, "I'm bad, Father. Please help me to be good," or "I want to be good more than anything in the world," or "I wonder if it's possible for me ever to be good again."

Goodness and peace. Peace and goodness. The more I meditated on the two words, the more I saw the connection between them and God. There is no peace without goodness, and there is no goodness without God.

I sometimes think that more than anything else people hunger for goodness, wanting to do the good thing, the right thing, even though it may cost them their lives.

Saint Maximilian Kolbe, the Franciscan priest-martyr killed at the Auschwitz concentration camp in 1941, gave an example of total goodness that cost him his life. The distraught father of a family was about to be executed. Kolbe volunteered to change places with him, sacrificing his life so that the innocent man could live and return to his family.

Why did he do it? Was he some kind of nut who didn't care about his own survival? Or was he a man who saw that something good had to be done and went ahead and did it without counting the cost?

Most of us think it was the latter. It was the right thing to do, so he did it.

The same is true of the young mother in Minneapolis who went through a wall of flame into her home to save her baby. Neither she nor the baby survived. Was it merely the powerful maternal instinct that drove her? Or was it because she knew it was the right thing, the good thing to do?

In spite of all appearances to the contrary, it may well be that the hunger for goodness is more basic than the most important human instincts, even more important than the will to live.

The philosophers tell us that evil itself is always sought under the guise of good. No one except the devil pursues evil as evil. We want goodness because we instinctively realize that we will have no peace without it. Goodness is the stuff that peace is made of. Trying to have peace without it would be like trying to swim without going into the water.

One of the beautiful things about the Church is that it has so many goodness-makers. The sacraments of Penance and the Eucharist are goodness-makers that have no equal. Many inactive Catholics return to the Church simply because they miss these sacraments so much.

As a confessor, I have wept tears of joy with penitents who found indescribable peace and profound comfort in the sacrament of Penance. As a minister of the Eucharist, I know well the peace that comes to those who are returning to the Lord after a long time away.

If you are ever to satisfy your craving for the peace that comes from doing good, you must continually place yourself in the hands of God.

Are You a Winner
or a Loser?

Are winners better people than losers? Should you even be concerned about winning or losing? Isn't it better that you just *get the job done* and let the chips fall where they may?

By some standards, Jesus Christ was a loser. So were two of his best friends. Jesus died on a cross; both Peter and Paul suffered shameful deaths. On the surface, their deaths could hardly be called glorious triumphs.

Some people think that the fat, the ugly, the ignorant, the weak, the sick are losers, and that the slim, the smart, the strong, the healthy are winners. Jesus didn't think so. "God chose those whom the world considers absurd to shame the wise; he singled out the weak of this world to shame the strong. He chose the world's lowborn and despised, those who count for nothing, to reduce to nothing those who were something" (1 Corinthians 1:27-28).

One of the more common human tendencies is to judge others by standards that are hollow — beauty, talent, money, clothes, fame. But these are not reliable yardsticks because people are not equal in all things. As human beings, we all have equal rights. However, we are not equal in our talents and abilities.

Only in areas like work, love, laughter, tears, pain, and joy are we truly equal. Regardless of our limitations, these are roads on which any of us can walk and find happiness.

Those people who consider themselves losers do so because they *want* to feel that way. And they feel that way because of a sense of guilt that comes from sin. God has forgiven them, but they will not forgive themselves.

In my thirty-odd years of priesthood, I have dealt with many people who felt that God had never forgiven their sins. In their profound sense of guilt, they would not let God tell them that today they are good, that he loves them, that his Son Jesus is a loving, forgiving, personal

Savior. They would never make a list of all their good qualities, of all the good deeds they have done, of all the acts of virtue they have practiced, of all the love they have given away. No, most of them wanted to make a list only of their faults and failings. Part of the blame for this, I'm afraid, must rest with priests and ministers who, through the years, have emphasized the spiritually negative instead of the positive. And because of this, the people whom they advised have approached God through fear rather than through love.

Last week I was talking with a man who was absolutely convinced that he was not good, that he was a loser. He said: ''I have a son who is on drugs and an unmarried daughter who is pregnant. Where did I go wrong? Is God punishing me for my past sins? I know all of this is happening because I am no good.''

No words of mine could convince him that he was not a loser. When he left, I wondered, as I often have, why people want to punish themselves in this way. Don't they know that God forgives and forgets? Don't they realize that he wants them to get rid of those feelings of guilt? Don't they understand that such guilt will slowly destroy their self-love and leave them incapable of loving their neighbor?

The author of the First Letter of John writes,

''See what love the Father has bestowed on us
in letting us be called children of God!
Yet that is what we are'' (1 John 3:1).

Since we are children, we can expect marvelous things from his hands — better than from the hands of our parents. One day Jesus spoke these words specifically to the parents among his listeners: ''If you, with all your sins, know how to give your children good things, how much more will the heavenly Father give the Holy Spirit to those who ask him'' (Luke 11:13). We can't lose with the Holy Spirit on our side.

All of us are winners in the eyes of God if we continue to care enough to love. And if we seem to lack that at times, we need only make an ardent desire to try, leaving the rest up to God who wants everyone to be a winner.

Are You
a "Counter"?

Our young pastor looked discouraged. I said to him, "Chuck, how'd the meeting go?"

"Not too good," he said. "Not many showed up. I wish there had been more."

"Who's counting?" I said.

"You're right. We're always counting, aren't we?" And with that we began a discussion about how people tend to measure results by the number in attendance.

In this sense, "counting" is practically synonymous with expecting successes, judging outcomes, totaling rewards. It means doing something and expecting something back. It means doing exactly what Jesus told us *not* to do: "Look at the birds in the sky. They do not sow or reap, they gather nothing into barns; yet your heavenly Father feeds them. . . . Learn a lesson from the way the wild flowers grow. They do not work; they do not spin. Yet I assure you, not even Solomon in all his splendor was arrayed like one of these" (Matthew 6:26,28-29).

Jesus was telling us to live our lives and do our jobs as well as we can and leave the rest to him. If we don't do that, he will say to us, "O weak in faith! Stop worrying . . . " (Matthew 6:30,31).

Our discussion that evening exposed a flaw in my faith. I was one who always wanted to be in control, to be sure of results, to receive a reward for my effort. What concerned me most was a desire for success — more for my own sake than for the Lord's.

I looked at my work with and for inactive Catholics and found I was always counting numbers and figuring percentages. I realized then that my ultimate success in my field depended entirely on God. My only obligation was to try to do my best.

In the years since that discussion, I have seen how the "stop counting" principle applies to many spheres of life: friendships, marriage, love, prayer, and work. There is no area to which the principle cannot be applied.

The other day I heard one woman tell another, "We've baby-sat five times for your kids. You've baby-sat only three times for us. You owe us two." Most of us live our lives along such principles. We live in a world where we want all things to come out even — although most of the time they don't. But how far do we go? At what point do we draw the line? When do we stop saying: I've done so much for you, now you must do so much for me?

If Jesus had been a "counter" he probably would have taken the betraying Peter, cut him up into little bits, and fed him to the fish. But we have no record of any such reaction. After the Resurrection, he treated Peter with great consideration and love.

One of the principles of the Genesis II program is this: "Live a life of love and mind your own business." This is hard to do because when we love we want love back, in full measure and overflowing — and God help those who do not return it . . . husbands, wives, children, friends, relatives, co-workers.

In my own life, once I ceased "counting," I began to feel free of many former tensions. My decision has eliminated the pettiness often found in human relationships. No longer do I wonder when others are going to "come across," "pay back," "do their part," "carry their weight." It feels good to stop "counting."

In the eyes of God, it doesn't matter whether you are successful or whether people thank you for what you do for them — as long as you always strive to do your best.

So stop "counting;" just keep on "doing."

Are You
a "Connector"?

The baby was perfect in every way — but she was born dead! The umbilical cord had wrapped around her neck and strangled her. For years, this husband and wife had been hoping and praying for a child. And now their hearts were broken. I have never seen people so sad and depressed. They had no other children and did not know if they could have any more. They had waited so long — and now this.

In my later conversations with this couple, I found out that they had lived together for several years before they were married. And they felt that this present sorrow was punishment for their past conduct.

I told them I did not think so. And we talked far into the night about "connecting" one event with another.

"Connecting" events in this sense is a presumption that some of us make: *This* happened in our lives because we did *that* some time ago. We seem to have a natural tendency to presume connections where there are none — connections that are probably the farthest things from the mind of God.

When people jump to such conclusions, I always ask "How do you know? Did an angel come down and tell you, or did you get a letter from God?" True, there were many "connected" events in the Old Testament — the expulsion of Adam and Eve (because of original sin), and the Flood (because of personal sin) are examples — but it was clear that these events were God's work as he himself revealed. We must be very reluctant to make such connections unless God reveals them.

Part of what is involved here is the fact that often forgiven sinners feel they have not done enough penance for their sins and now God is making them pay in some way or other.

These people *want* to be punished. This attitude is regrettable because the hundreds of daily pains, aches, disappointments, shocks, betrayals, and sicknesses can be the primary means of restoring the balance that sin has disturbed. There is no need, then, to resort to "connecting" events."

I think we priests and ministers are at least partially responsible for this "connection" syndrome. A few weeks ago a woman told me that a priest said her cancer was a punishment by God for not being married in the Church. I shuddered. I told her not to believe the words of the priest; they were obviously a pathetic exploitation of fear.

God doesn't keep book on us. He's not up there in heaven mulling over a long list of our sins and failings. With God we basically have no past — we have only NOW. What God cares about is who we are *now,* whether we love him *now,* and whether we are trying our best *now.*

This is the only conclusion we can draw from the way Jesus lived, dined, and walked with sinners. "While Jesus was at table in Matthew's home, many tax collectors and those known as sinners came to join Jesus and his disciples at dinner" (Matthew 9:10). Later Matthew says that not only did Jesus eat with sinners, he loved them (see Matthew 11:19). In no place do we find Jesus castigating forgiven sinners and reminding them that they had once sinned. He certainly did not do this with Magdalen, and he did not do it with Peter. Jesus is the friend of forgiven sinners and is not about to punish them any more than they have punished themselves; sin, after all, is by itself one of its own worst punishments.

The young parents mentioned in the opening paragraph eventually came to accept the fact that God was not punishing them for their sins with the death of their child. And today they have two lovely children, a boy and a girl.

Are You
a Victim of Pride?

When I was a missionary on the Amazon River in Brazil, I was assigned to minister to people who lived out in the jungle itself, away from the established settlement. To reach my people required the aid of a motorboat with a top speed of five miles an hour. The motor was always breaking down. This was particularly frustrating to me because I had neither the skill nor the dexterity to repair the thing.

Once, after a month-long journey into the jungle, I was especially anxious to get back to my confreres and a more civilized lifestyle. The boat boy and I tried for hours to get the motor started. Finally I said to myself, "I am a priest. I believe in prayer. I'll pray over it."

Then I got out my surplice, stole, holy water, and book, and I prayed for the "healing" of the motor.

Nothing happened.

I prayed some more.

Still nothing.

Then I put aside my religious gear, went to the back of the boat, and kicked the motor. That did nothing but hurt my foot.

On that occasion, as on countless others, I took the failure personally. I looked on myself as the victim of another defeat.

I wanted things to go my way. I didn't want that motor or anything or anybody to give me trouble, to keep me from my goal.

Oh, I know that I am imperfect, that other people are imperfect, that boat motors are imperfect. In fact, everything, with the exception of God, is imperfect. But when too much imperfection rises up to strike me, I get that old "Why-does-this-have-to-happen-to-me?" reaction.

I also let myself be victimized by people. When I come face-to-face with someone who has a superior attitude, it makes me feel inferior. Even when I know that his or her attitude is only insecurity hiding behind a facade of superiority, I feel diminished. I feel victimized.

Pride, of course, is at the bottom of all this. Like an insidious serpent, it whispers: "You don't have to take anything from anybody. You're *You* with an upper case Y. Now go out there and get angry if things don't go your way!"

It is pride that robs me of one of my most precious possessions — freedom to choose my mood for the moment. And because of this I allow people's lack of consideration, their insensitivity, their clumsiness, their carelessness, their injustice to break the back of my happiness.

I am beginning to understand why Jesus said that those who are humble will be exalted. The humble have fewer expectations. They don't think the world owes them a living. They don't have to succeed at everything they do. They don't have to win every game.

I'm learning that the humble — like baseball hitters — have only to bat .300, not a perfect 1.000, to be considered good hitters. They are realistic about themselves and life and love.

I'm learning that most humble people can face insults, and not allow setbacks to discourage them immoderately. They are good examples of what is meant by the words: "When you're sleeping on the floor, no one can throw you out of bed."

I'm also learning that humility makes for patience. Humble people have the ability to accept the imperfections of this life. They work patiently to overcome their weaknesses, not allowing them to dictate the quality of their lives.

I'm still learning.

Last week, a man pulled into my parking spot just as I was getting ready to back in. "So what?" I said to myself, "I'll find another spot."

I refused to let myself become a victim of pride. And with God's help you can do the same.

Are You
a Faceless One?

The ugly
The deformed
The uncouth, the unwanted and the unneeded
The annoyers
The little-minded
The cowards
The army of the awkward:

These I salute,
    And all their kin.

Not criminals
Not sinners,
I speak to the faceless ones,
And I use the phrase with love.

Everyone wants a face,
Everyone wants to be recognized,
We all want to carve our names on the stone of the present
    and write them on the pages of history.
No one wants to be faceless,
Yet, in the strange riddle of life,
    facelessness is the common lot.

Is God, then, unjust?
No.

Each person is different.
Each one is a closed world.
We all have our own sun, stars, and moon.

We all have our own inner greatness.

The size of the sun and stars and moon
   is not important.
Nor important, the beauty of the light they give.
It is important that they be there.

The same is true of all persons.
Unequal are we in these areas:
In beauty and in talent
In courage and in ability.
Equal are we in these:
In pain and in tears
In laughter and in God.

The faceless ones should know:
That outward greatness is a fearful burden
   and ofttimes a door which shuts out happiness.
The great ones are to be prayed for,
   not envied.

The faceless ones are to be pitied,
   if they curse their limitations,
   trying to daydream themselves into greatness,
   not understanding that they were carefully made
   by divine hands,
      which lovingly await their return.

To faceless ones, there is challenge here.
They should recognize this fact:
The truly great are those
   who do the best they can with what they have.

Rather than praise the faceless ones
I challenge them to do what they can
   to change the face of the earth.

Why Do You Let
Little Things Bother You?

Pretend for a moment that you are Napoleon coming home from the wars. You fought each battle with great skill — and you won. You saved your country.

The people — waving banners and tossing bouquets — are lined up by the thousands along the streets to welcome you home. A grateful nation has spared no expense to show appreciation for what you have done.

But in the midst of the tumultuous crowd you see one man who is neither waving nor cheering. He is looking at you with no expression at all. He seems unimpressed with you and with what you have done.

The victory parade continues. You salute and wave and smile. But in the back of your mind lurks the question: Why didn't that one man wave like everyone else?

Does any of this seem familiar to you? Have you ever been in a situation where you let the lack of one small word, gesture, or deed of no great consequence ruin your day?

I have. And I kept wondering how I could be so dumb as to let it happen.

One such occasion was the day of my ordination. It was a long-awaited and eagerly anticipated culmination of my years of study and training. But I let it be ruined in part because I was irritated by the slow service at the ordination banquet. Everything — in my judgment — was supposed to be perfect on my ordination day (emphasis on the word *my*).

A young bride told me she let her wedding day be ruined by her aggravation at the priest who performed the ceremony. (Father was wearing dirty, muddy shoes.)

One of my parishioners once told me I ruined his Sunday because I did not shake hands with him as he was leaving the church. He said, ''You shook hands with everyone else but not with me.'' He wouldn't accept my explanation that I have restricted vision difficulties and most likely did not see him.

Why do we let little things bother us?

It may be our pride. Do we think so highly of ourselves that we feel everything has to turn out the way we want it, or else? Are we still small children who keep saying to life, "If you don't play the game by my rules, I'll take my ball and go home?"

Again, it may be that our expectations are too high. Do we want too much out of people, out of life? Does everything have to be black and white, clear-cut, neatly packaged, perfectly just, totally considerate, completely reasonable, always on time?

To help solve this problem, let's ask ourselves another question. If we had perfect control over our lives and if everything was done and happened in the ways described above, would we be any happier?

Actually, we would probably be bored to death, like the perfect golfer with the perfect swing who never makes a mistake and never shoots anything over par. Dullsville!

Why do we let little things bother us?

The most honest answer to that question is that we are all a little bit crazy. We are sufficiently paranoid that we create enemies where there are none; we tilt at windmills that do not exist; we make mountains out of molehills.

When we find ourselves being bothered by our lack of control over the details of our lives, it's a good idea to remember a person named Jesus. His life was under the control of his Father. His destiny was in the hands of that Father, whose will he had come to fulfill.

Our own lives and destinies are also in the hands of the Father. We know from the testimony of his Son how much he loves us. And that looms large enough to outweigh all those *little things* that threaten to bother us everyday.

GUIDELINES

No Change,
No Growth

"My Church used to be a rock. Now it's sand!"

"If the Church is divine, how can it change? God doesn't change."

"I hate change — in my job, in my family, and in my Church."

These comments were made at a Forum for Inactive Catholics. The Forum is an opportunity for Catholics who no longer practice their faith to get together with a priest and discuss their feelings about God, the Church, and themselves.

Many of the participants said that the main reason they no longer practice their faith is because of recent changes in the Church. These changes have upset them, made them feel strange, even unwanted.

It's easy to sympathize with them because it is not easy to change. Sometimes it feels like a stripping process. As one woman said, "Change leaves me so exposed."

The business world practices an adage which reads: "Grow or die." This is also true in other areas of life: There can be no growth without change, and there can be neither change nor growth without openness to change.

Note the growth that followed from the changes made by these three personages in the Bible:

Amos was told by the priest of Bethel to go to the land of Judah and earn his bread there by prophesying. He answered that he was no prophet, only "a shepherd and a dresser of sycamores." But the Lord said, "Go, prophesy to my people Israel" and Amos did (see Amos 7:10-15).

The Lord appointed Jeremiah to be " . . . a prophet to the nations." Jeremiah argued that he did not know how to speak, that he was too young. And the Lord answered:

"Say not, 'I am too young.'
     To whomever I send you, you shall go"
(see Jeremiah 1:5-7).

A young Jewish maiden named Mary was betrothed to a man named Joseph and presumably would become the mother of a large family as was the custom of her people. But one day an angel appeared to her and asked if she would be willing to become the Mother of Jesus the Savior. And, although this meant that she would have to change her way of life, she said yes. Her acceptance changed the course of history and inaugurated the growth of Christianity.

In many ways change is the name of the game. It always precedes the growth that surrounds us on every side. Radio, TV, jet planes, computers, and satellites are only a few of the changes that have modified our lives in this century. We live with these changes and take them for granted.

The Second Vatican Council was the Church's answer to a changing world, just as the Council of Trent in the sixteenth century was an answer to the challenges presented by the Protestant Reformation. Growth took place in the Church after the changes mandated by Trent; and growth continues in the Church today because of the changes made by Vatican II. Most people will agree with that statement, and all persons will do so once they begin to feel more at home with change.

Change, then, requires trust. It means moving into the unknown, the unfamiliar. It means closing our eyes and taking the plunge as did Amos and Jeremiah and Mary.

The Genesis II program reminds us that "lack of trust is the biggest reason for a lack of sanctity in the world today." Only when we run the risk of trusting can we make the changes that result in growth. Believe it: There is no growth without change.

Heed
God's Signals

Has anyone ever said to you: "What do I have to do to get your attention?"

It's a question parents sometimes hear from their teenagers. It's a question teenagers frequently hear from their parents, and married people hear from their spouses. It's a question many friends would like to ask but don't. They are afraid of getting into a hassle.

The question is important because it is really asking: "Are you taking me for granted? Do you know that I am here and that I am important? Do you recognize my value as a person or am I just an object in your life?"

We can imagine that God must ask of us the same question: What do I have to do to get your attention?

God does not want to be taken for granted. He doesn't want to be thought of as only an aspirin when we are in pain or a convenience item from the corner store when we are in need. He doesn't want to be considered a fringe benefit that comes with the covenant made with him at Baptism.

God wants to be recognized as a real person who loves us; he wants to keep up a good, loving relationship with us. But he will not force his love on us. Forced love is rape, not love.

Like any lover, God sends out various signals to get our attention. These signals may be thoughts that come to us in prayer, doubts that cross our minds, inspirations that arise at Mass, ideas that strike us during a homily.

These signals may also be sensed in the aftermath of pain and tragedy. God does not cause the pain and the tragedy but he does use them to draw us closer to him. He utilizes them to get our attention.

God got my attention one day:

When I was in the eighth grade, I somehow became convinced that my parents hated me, that the Church was no good, and that God was mean. So I decided to do something bad, like sin. The worst sin I could think of was to miss Mass on Sunday. So I did. As I rode my bicycle by the church just as the kids were going in for the children's Mass, I thought to myself how stupid they were. Fifteen minutes later, I changed my mind.

I was holding on to the back of a truck, trying to get a free ride, when the driver made a sharp right turn which threw me under the body of the truck. I narrowly missed being run over. The only damage done was to an elbow and to my clothes. As soon as I recovered — my conscience now alerted — I hustled back to the church like the devil was after me (I felt sure he was) and attended three Masses. Never before had I been so pious. God had indeed gotten my attention.

God tried to get the attention of Pharaoh in the Old Testament, to free his people from the land of Egypt. Pharaoh would not let them go. So God turned the rivers into blood. When that didn't work, he sent a plague of gnats, then flies. God had to send a total of ten plagues before Pharaoh finally realized that the Lord meant business.

Religion is a serious business because it is all about love — the love between God and his people. And love is not to be taken lightly; it must not be taken for granted. It is a good and holy thing to be open to the signals that love keeps sending. So, be convinced that God loves you so much that he will always be trying to get your attention. Therefore, when you recognize his signals, heed them.

Learn
From the Rose

2❧ One summer day the wind blew hard,
   Scattering leaves in all its fury,
   Bruising and breaking all my flowers,
   Damaging the stem of one of my roses,
   Forming teardrops of pain from its fallen petals.

2❧ I asked the rose, its stem all broken:
   Why must you lose your lovely petals?
   Why must your beauty fade?

2❧ The rose answered:
   I knew my petals would eventually fall.
   I knew my beauty would soon fade away,
   So I asked the rose-maker
   Why must I be bruised and broken?
   I have joy to share and beauty to give.

2❧ And the rose-maker answered:
   Before I fashioned the sun and the moon
   And formed the land-encircled waters,
   I molded you within my mind.
   Your spark of joy
   And gift of beauty
   I laced with measures of pain.

2❧ Why the pain? I asked.
   Am I your enemy?

2❧ You are not my enemy.
   You are my friend.
   Your pain, like that of all creatures,
   Is planted there by me your Maker.

&. See for yourself,
   O spark of joy and gift of beauty,
   What needs you have:
      You thirst for water.
      You die without soil.
      You fade with too much sun.
   By yourself you cannot stand.

&. Yes, rose-maker, the wind proved that.
   And I see that I am not perfect.
   But I still don't fathom the reason for pain.

&. My plan for pain is a loving one.
   I weigh all pain with tender care,
   And only when it targets love,
   Do I set it free.

&. There is more, rose — much more.
   I speak of mystery.
   If you solved my mystery,
   If you knew my secret,
   You would be the rose-maker.
   That cannot be.
   There can be but one rose-maker.

&. If you knew all,
   There would be no need for trust,
   And my love would go begging.
   You might opt to part from me,
   But I do not want you to leave.
   I want you near because I love you.
   And without the mystery of pain
   That is impossible.

&. That, dear friend,
   is what the rose-maker told me.
   I believe him,
   Because he is good,
   He is wise,
   He is God.

Strive
for Goodness

As I grow older (middle sixties) and my hair becomes whiter and thinner (five hundred forty-one strands left), it frequently occurs to me that life's success is measured by the time spent in seeking it. Success is a result of careful planning and hard work. And that takes time.

To be successful in acquiring goodness demands time-consuming hard work, so I knew that I should not be angry with myself if success did not come immediately.

During my lifetime, I have worked with three kinds of time: God's, the other person's, and mine. I was particularly fond of mine.

My sense of time, however, was not necessarily perfect. It was hurried, insensitive, impatient. It wanted instant results. But it was mine and I liked it.

I was much like the person who told God, "Lord, give me the gift of patience — and give it to me right now!"

Then the Holy Spirit sent a charming elderly lady into my life.

One night I was talking to a group of active Catholics about those who are inactive, those who do not come to church anymore. I explained that we should not pressure them, that we should welcome them sincerely and then let them proceed at their own pace. I told them that God has his own timetable.

"That's true," said our charming friend. "It took me fifty-five years."

We were all stunned when we heard those words, and a holy silence fell upon us as we tried to absorb the implication of what she had said.

> "There is an appointed time for everything,
> and a time for every affair under the heavens"
> (Ecclesiastes 3:1).

This was certainly true of the lady in question.

As I looked at her serene countenance, I remembered the words of Psalm 34:9: "Taste and see how good the LORD is." And I likewise recalled how the First Letter of Peter exhorted the newly baptized to growth in holiness now that they had "tasted that the Lord is good" (1 Peter 2:3).

That she had tasted of the Lord's goodness was evident. But where did she find his goodness? In people, of course, and in her prayers and in her love.

God puts a tremendous amount of goodness in his people, and it is our job to find and savor it. We can find it by listening to the soul-beats of others, sharing their pain, building better bridges to cross over into their hearts. We can savor it by not taking other human beings for granted. It is then that we discover the goodness of the Lord (his grace freely given). And once we taste of it, we begin to grow in holiness.

We too must let our own goodness show. People have a right to know how good God has been to us so they can participate in his goodness. Hence the value of gatherings such as Bible studies, Renew groups, prayer meetings, and charismatic renewals. In and through such groups, both human and divine goodness will manifest themselves for the benefit of all.

And this goodness will be ours if we open ourselves to the Spirit who will persuade us to taste delights hitherto unknown. He will help us overcome our natural tendency to look for the bad in others rather than the good.

It takes time to achieve goodness, but the effort is more than worthwhile.

Be Affirming

He approached me from the back, put his hand gently on my shoulder, and said, "A very good morning to you, Bill."

I turned to him and said, "It's better than when it started."

"What do you mean by that?" he asked.

I explained, "Before you greeted me so cordially I was feeling depressed, blue, down in the dumps. Then you came along and changed my mood. I feel better, reassured."

My friend had just affirmed me. He said that he knew I was there, that he was interested enough in me to reach out to me.

Over the years I have witnessed the tremendous power of affirmation. I have seen it change people in seemingly miraculous ways. It creates "a new person."

Affirmation means reaching out to others to let them know that you know they are there and are glad that they are. It means letting them know you are concerned or worried about them or that you need them or love them. It is a bridge that unites people for the betterment of all.

A husband told me recently, "We were heading for a divorce — no doubt about it. Then I came home from the office one day, looked at my wife, and saw big questions in her eyes. I walked over to her and put my arms around her. We didn't talk. Our tears did. How long we cried I don't know. Then we started talking as we never had talked before. . . . There was no divorce."

They both reached out and a new union was forged.

Sometimes we do not want to affirm others. We are slow to reach out. Why? One big reason is competition.

In varied ways, most of us are competing in the game of happiness. We want to be Number One Happy Person. We don't want our neighbor or our sister-in-law to be happier than we are.

Affirmation is a Gospel way to give away our life (see Mark 8:35). If we keep it all for ourselves, we die.

We see that in Jesus' life. His whole existence as a human being was an affirmation. Basically he came to say we are important enough and lovable enough to make him take on human flesh and give his whole life for us.

The most difficult part of affirmation is simply deciding to do so. We are hampered by liberal amounts of jealousy and selfishness. "Why should I congratulate the person who got the promotion I was trying so hard to get?"

But promoted or not, successful or not, powerful or not, beautiful or not, rich or not — we all need daily doses of affirmation. Nobody in this life has it made. We are all prone to failure and are in urgent need of help from other human beings.

Opportunities for affirmation are as numerous as the people we meet and the avenues of practicing it are many. We can affirm in the following ways:

a) *By praising or complimenting*. But we must be sincere.

b) *By touching*. Shaking hands, hugging, or kissing are examples.

c) *By being there*. Physical presence alone can be a great comfort when words or gestures are empty.

d) *By listening*. We truly hear not only with the ear but also with the eye, the mind, and the heart. We *listen* to the whole person.

e) *By being compassionate*. We walk into another's brokenness and help him or her put the pieces back together again.

f) *By sharing ourselves*. To share with another our own fears and failures, joys and successes is an affirmation of value; it says, "I trust you enough to let you know who I am."

Affirmation can "create" a new *other*. And while it is doing so, it can create a new *you*.

Sex: Follow Its
Sacred Path

What are you, sex?

Diamond with a thousand lovely facets?
Or cheap glass shattered into countless splinters?
Are you wine?
Or gall?

Or are you a mixture of all these things and more:
So complex that only Divinity knows your essence?

You are a billowing sea, a parched desert,
A cragged mountain, a bottomless pit.

You are close at hand:
So near, and yet so far away.

We reach for you and you are smoke.
We flee from you and you are steel.

Are you in the mind?
Or in the marrow?
Or in both?

In the catalogue of instincts
They place you second.
Mere living comes first.

You populate.
You decimate.
You create.
You annihilate.

You die a thousand deaths,
You live again a million.

You are a Christmas,
A Calvary.
An Easter.

Beauty becomes you
Like music writ by Master hand.
Its final song espouses godly ends
By blending, with ecstatic pleasure,
Acts that bring forth life.

But some make you
Mere flower in a harlot's tresses,
Plucked only at the urge of passion,
Leaving kingdom ravaged,
Reason bankrupt,
Right wronged.

So many times misused
By those who do not have the right,
You have errantly become
For those with right
A tarnished tool.

Is it not true, sex,
That when love opens body's door
You fly to spirit's realms
Where souls are fused?

Is not your climax
A groping,
Not only for body
And for soul,
But also for God?

Whatever else be true,
This is verity itself:
You are a sacred path
On which Adam's heirs can walk
To God.

Take Care
of the Dying

Give ear to this story about a raw, heart-wrenching incident in the life of an American priest working for derelict souls on the edge of the jungle in Brazil:

"Padre?"

"Yes?"

"Will you come with me?"

"What's up?"

"To bless a body."

"Who died?"

"That man you prayed with yesterday. Remember?"

I remembered. He was a man of 70 years, toothpick thin, yellow as a lemon, agonizing from within and from without.

"Are you another daughter?"

"Yeah."

"Why did you let him die like that?"

"He was too old to work. Always complaining."

"You should take care of the dying, no matter what."

She shrugged her shoulders.

I got my sick call outfit and went off with her in the hot morning sun.

Vila da Barca (Villa of the Boats) was our destination. The place could hardly be called a villa in the American sense of the word. To us Redemptorist priests working in this city of Belem in jungled northeastern Brazil, it means a vast, swamp-like, festering hole where thousands of souls are jammed together in incredible squalor and misery. It means a place where murder, rape, incest, and stealing are more the order of the day than cooking, cleaning, eating, and sleeping. We Redemptorists live right on the edge of this swamp.

I followed the girl to the house. We walked on boardwalks set upon stilts. The walks are shaky and unreliable at their best. At this time of the year, they're very bad. The people rip up the boards to use as firewood for cooking. Then they scream to the city authorities that nothing is done to maintain the walks.

I weigh 210 pounds, so I have to watch my step. The area is flooded by the tides, and a slip means plunging into unspeakable filth.

We walked gingerly along, passing row after row of thatchroofed hovels. Pigs, dogs, chickens, and cats live with the people.

At practically every step people call out: "Benção, *Padre.*" I bless them.

In ten minutes we're at the house. It's jammed with raucous folk. Four men are playing cards right next to the crude coffin; I ask them quietly: "Don't you respect the dead?"

When they refused to answer I shouted at them: "Stop the play or I'll throw you out the window."

At this, they picked up their cards and stood up, making no more trouble.

The man had been dead about fifteen hours. There is no embalming here. I seemed to be the only one who noticed the terrible stench.

I opened the ritual and read the services for the dead. That finished, I asked the mourners to join me in some Our Fathers and Hail Marys for the dead man.

It was a good time for an instruction on death. I said a few words on praying for the deceased, reminding them that our turn will come, that we should all be prepared. No one paid much attention. Nevertheless I went on:

"Look on the body of this man and see in him a picture of your own death."

From a corner of the room came a voice: "Padre, we of *Vila da Barca* are already dead."

I gasped. Those words cut at my heart like a dagger. I have never heard anything that so accurately described the life of these people.

When I regained control I said: "God bless all of you, especially the family. God bless the card players."

I gathered up my religious gear and left the house. There was not a dry piece of clothing on me.

Walk
With Jesus

Once upon a time there was a man, a man with scars. And a girl, a girl with dreams.

The man with scars came to the girl with dreams and said to her: I love you. Come away with me.

The girl with dreams said: I have thought on one such as you. Are you the one for whom I have waited? Are you the one of whom I have dreamed?

The man with scars said: I am the one.

The girl said: I see that you are beautiful. But you have scars.

The man said: Do not let my scars frighten you. Do not even be frightened when I tell you that if you come away with me you will have scars too.

The girl said: But I would be frightened. Scars would make me unhappy.

The man said: Not mine. To you they will be bittersweet.

The girl said: I do not know if I love *you*.

The man said: Trust me.

The girl said: I will trust you. I will go away with you.

She went away with him.

Together they traveled far.

They walked over hot deserts. They tiptoed over deep oceans. They climbed high mountains and they ranged through verdant valleys.

Wherever they walked a great lady walked with them. When the girl with dreams stumbled, the great lady took her hand and helped her.

Yes, together they walked far.

Mostly they walked with children. They walked in the ringing laughter of the little ones. They walked in their absurd tears. With cautious step, even though they were big, they walked into the tiny hearts of the children. When they walked out they left gifts behind —

splendid gifts, beautiful gifts. This made the man with scars and the great lady very happy. It made the girl with dreams happy too.

They walked with the sick and the old and the poor and the needy. Indeed, no class or type of people escaped their attention.

At times the girl with dreams said to the man with scars: I am tired. I will walk no more with you.

He said to her: We have come far. We have yet far to go. Do not falter now. Clasp my hand more tightly. Close your eyes. Trust me.

She trusted him, not letting go of his hand. She shut her eyes. Suddenly she was not so tired. Abruptly the road became smoother. And when she opened her eyes she saw his scars upon her.

He said: Is the pain too great?

She said: No, not too great. I know now what you meant when you said that they would be bittersweet.

He said: True travelers must learn to bear my scars . . . . Let us go on.

They traveled on. They walked over more hot deserts. Again they tiptoed over deep oceans. They climbed other high mountains and ranged through other verdant valleys.

One day someone came up to the girl with dreams and said to her: I want to buy your scars.

She said: Why do you want to buy them?

He said: I do not like the man with scars. I do not want anyone to bear them. I want to erase all the scars which he has left around the world.

She said: I will not sell them.

He said: I will give you much money.

She said: That will not do.

He said: I will give you kingdoms.

She said: I don't need other kingdoms.

He said: What do you want?

She said: I want only to walk with him.

She went to the man with scars and put her hand in his and said: I love you.

He said: You have always loved me even when you were unaware of it.

They continued their journey.

Whenever and wherever they found hearts, they stopped and entered. And when they departed, they left gifts behind — splendid gifts, beautiful gifts.

Some hearts they could not enter. This saddened the girl with dreams.

The man with scars said to her: Be not sad. You can do only so much.

She said: I want to do more.

He said: I am happy that you want to do more.

Then, one great day they came to a milestone.

He said: Let us pause and rest.

They rested.

While they were resting, people arrived. And from the people came a spokesman.

The spokesman said: You have traveled far. You have come to the milestone.

The girl with dreams said: Yes, I see that we have come a great distance. It does not seem that we have traveled this far.

The spokesman said: Today is a very great day, and we are pleased that you have come to the milestone.

She said: I am pleased too.

The spokesman said: I want to thank you for having walked so far with him.

The girl with dreams said: Do not thank me. Thank him.

The spokesman said: Did you walk alone with him?

She said: No, a great lady walked with us. She encouraged me immensely.

The spokesman said: The man with scars is a very great man. I am pleased that you have walked with him.

The girl with dreams said: I am very happy that I have walked with him these many years. I trust that many more will walk with him in the future.

By the same author . . .

HOW TO REACH OUT TO INACTIVE CATHOLICS
A Practical Parish Program

Developed over a three-year period by Father McKee, this successful program offers any parish priest a practical approach to reaching those Catholics who have grown away from the Church. The book includes a complete outline of the program and the step-by-step instructions necessary to reach out to more than 12 million inactive Catholics in the United States today. **$6.95**

More inspirational titles from Liguori Publications

60 WAYS TO LET YOURSELF GROW
by Martha Mary McGaw, C.S.J.

A happy, exciting book that shows how to make the most of the precious gift of life — everyday! Each page presents an idea or suggestion to help the reader grow, blossom, open up to life — and includes free space for personal notes. **$1.50**

GROWTH THROUGH VIRTUE
Month by Month With St. Alphonsus Liguori
by Daniel L. Lowery, C.SS.R.

In these pages, St. Alphonsus Liguori's classic **Virtue of the Month** program has been updated for today's Christian. Focusing on a separate virtue for each month, it offers a sound opportunity for spiritual growth through prayer, reading, and reflection on basic Christian qualities. **$1.50**

BECOMING A NEW PERSON
Twelve Steps to Christian Growth
by Philip St. Romain

Based on the same twelve-step plan used to free people from obsessive-compulsive behavior (drugs, alcohol, etc.) this book offers ''healthy'' people a way to break free in their spiritual life . . . to become better and happier . . . to become a NEW PERSON. **$2.95**